Bible Stories for....
Early Readers

Level 2
Book 5

Jonah's Ride
Jonah 1-3

By Lavaun Linde
Mary Quishenberry
Illustrated by
Joe Maniscalco

"I have a place
I want you to go,"
God tells Jonah.
"It is full of men with sin.
Go and help them to love Me."

"I do not want
to do that job."
Jonah runs
and gets on a boat.
"I will get in this spot
to ride and hide
from God."
But Jonah
can not hide
from God.

All goes well,
till God sends a bad wind.
The boat tips from side to side,
as the waves rise and rise!!
The men in the boat
do not feel safe!!

The men bow down
to fake gods and beg,
"Help us now!"
But the boat still tips
from side to side
as the waves rise and rise.
The men see
that the fake gods
are of no help.

"Quick! Get the big bags and toss them."

The men toss lots and lots
into the sea,
but the men
do not feel safe yet.

The man that runs the boat
yells to Jonah,
"Wake up!
This is no time to sleep!
Get up and ask your God
to save us!"

Jonah gets up.

Jonah tells the men on the boat,
"I am the blame for the bad wind
and the big waves.
Toss me in to the sea
and my God will stop the wind
and the waves."

The men in the boat pray to Jonah's God, "Thank You, God. Thank You."

God loves Jonah
and sends a BIG FISH
to keep Jonah safe
in the sea.

Jonah rides and prays the rest of the day.

"God, save me!
I do not like
to ride inside this fish!"
Jonah rides and prays
all the next day.

"God, I love You!
I do not want
to ride and hide this way."
Jonah rides and prays
for three days.

God makes the BIG FISH
spit up Jonah onto the shore.

God tells Jonah,
"I love you,
and I still have the job
in that place
for you to do."

Jonah is glad
to do the job for God.
And best of all,
all the men in that place
get rid of sin.

God has a promise
for me in Joshua 1:9.

Something to Think About

1. Why did Jonah get on the boat?
2. How did Jonah feel about being inside the BIG FISH?
3. What kind of job does God have for me to do?